SEWER GATORS

This series features unsolved mysteries, urban legends, and other curious stories. Each creepy, shocking, or befuddling book focuses on what people believe and hear. True or not? That's for you to decide!

45th Parallel Press

Published in the United States of America by Cherry Lake Publishing
Ann Arbor, Michigan
www.cherrylakepublishing.com

Author: Virginia Loh-Hagan
Reading Adviser: Marla Conn MS, Ed., Literacy specialist, Read-Ability, Inc.
Book Designer: Felicia Macheske

Photo Credits: © Vladimir Mulder/Shutterstock.com, cover; © Andrea Izzotti/Shutterstock.com, cover; © bleung/
Shutterstock.com, 5; © Ron Rowan Photography/Shutterstock.com, 7; © RaquelBagnol/Shutterstock.com, 8;
© Matthew Orselli/Shutterstock.com, 11; © reptiles4all/Shutterstock.com, 13; © Everett Collection/
Shutterstock.com, 15; © Jaromir Chalabala/Shutterstock.com, 16; © J Walters/Shutterstock.com, 18; © Thomas
W. Woodruff/Shutterstock.com, 21; © Marcos Mesa Sam Wordley/Shutterstock.com, 22; © photoBeard/
Shutterstock.com, 25; © LightTheBox/Shutterstock.com, 26; © Benjamin Simeneta/Shutterstock.com, 29

Graphic Elements Throughout: © iofoto/Shutterstock.com; © COLCU/Shutterstock.com; © spacedrone808/
Shutterstock.com; © rf.vector.stock/Shutterstock.com; © donatas1205/Shutterstock.com; © cluckva/
Shutterstock.com; © Eky Studio/Shutterstock.com

45th Parallel Press is an imprint of Cherry Lake Publishing.

Library of Congress Cataloging-in-Publication Data

Names: Loh-Hagan, Virginia, author.
Title: Sewer gators / by Dr. Virginia Loh-Hagan.
Description: Ann Arbor : Cherry Lake Publishing, 2018. | Series: Urban
Legends: don't read alone! | Audience: Grade 4 to 6. | Includes
bibliographical references and index.
Identifiers: LCCN 2017035396| ISBN 9781534107632 (hardcover) | ISBN
9781534109612 (pdf) | ISBN 9781534108622 (pbk.) | ISBN 9781534120600
(hosted ebook)
Subjects: LCSH: Alligators—Juvenile literature. | Urban folklore—Juvenile
literature.
Classification: LCC QL666.C925 L64 2018 | DDC 597.98/4—dc23
LC record available at https://lccn.loc.gov/2017035396

Cherry Lake Publishing would like to acknowledge the work of The Partnership for 21st Century Skills.
Please visit www.p21.org for more information.

Printed in the United States of America
Corporate Graphics

TABLE OF CONTENTS

Chapter One

SCALY SIGHTINGS

What are some actual gator sightings in New York City?

In 2001, people reported seeing an alligator in Central Park. Central Park is in New York City. About 24 people saw the alligator in a lake. Charles G. Sturcken is a city worker. He said the alligator should be taken to the **sewers**. Sewers are underground pipes or tunnels. They carry away wastewater. Sturcken said, "The sewer system is much warmer and is the city's answer to a natural swamp."

Tina Bailey came from Florida. She wanted to catch the alligator. Her husband is a professional alligator wrestler. Bailey put her hand in the water. She grabbed its head. The "Central Park Alligator" was 2 feet (61 centimeters) long. It turned out to be a **caiman**. Caimans are crocodiles. They're related to alligators.

A caimon was found in Central Park's Harlem Meer.

CONSIDER THE
EVIDENCE

Caimans are smaller than alligators. They can grow to be about 7 feet (2 meters) long. They're more likely to be in sewers than alligators. They're bought as pets more often than alligators. But they're illegal in the United States. Illegal means against the law. Caimans are smuggled into the country all the time. Smuggled means to sneak in. Caimans have long snouts. A snout is the mouth and nose area. Caimans have small, yellow eyes. They can live in both saltwater and freshwater. Alligators only live in freshwater. Caimans are more hostile. They bite. They're quick to attack. Alligators are less likely to attack humans. They only attack when triggered. But "sewer gators" is more fun to say than "sewer caimans"!

Another caiman was found in November 2006. This one was found in Brooklyn. Brooklyn is in New York City. The caiman was outside an apartment building.

Anthony Stevens was guarding the area. He thought he saw a baby alligator. The creature was 15 inches (38 cm) long. It was resting in a pile of leaves.

Cops got a call on the radio. They heard, "There's an alligator in the rear!" Six cops rushed to help Stevens. They tried to catch the caiman. They grabbed its tail. The caiman "snapped and hissed." The cops used a shoelace to tie its mouth shut.

Most wild animals found in cities are sent to wildlife parks.

Caimans and alligators are not supposed to be in New York City.

In August 2010, a caiman was caught in Queens. Queens is also in New York City. The caiman was hiding under a parked blue car.

Joyce Hackett saw the caiman. She said, "It was about 2 feet long. It was like the urban legend washes up from the sewer and says, 'What the heck am I doing here?' and hides under a Datsun."

Cops caught the caiman with a rope. They closed its mouth with tape. James Duffy is a cop. He said, "It's a big mystery. It could have been dumped from a car. Or it could have come out of a sewer."

Chapter Two

URBAN SWAMP MONSTERS

How did alligators get into sewers? What are sewer gators?

Stories about seeing caimans and alligators in New York City are exciting. They remind people of urban legends about sewer **gators**. Gator is short for alligator. New York City is famous for many things. There's the Empire State Building. There's the Statue of Liberty. And there are sewer gators! Some people believe that alligators live in the sewers.

Sewers are dark. They're scary. They're perfect places for urban swamp monsters. Rich New Yorkers went on vacation to Florida. They bought baby alligators. They gave them to their children for pets. They lost interest in the alligators. They flushed them down their toilet.

Alligators are common in Florida.

BIOGRAPHY

The New York City Department of Environmental Protection is in charge of the city's sewer system. The city has 7,400 miles (11,909 kilometers) of sewer pipes. The sewers flush 1.3 billion gallons (5 billion liters) of water every day. Emily Lloyd was the department's commissioner. Commissioner means boss. Lloyd retired in 2017. She said, "Every single day we work to provide critical services—such as high-quality drinking water—that allows the city to grow and thrive." Lloyd helped build better sewer systems. The mayor said, "Commissioner Lloyd always had the health of New Yorkers and the environment in mind with the work she helped lead."

The gators learned to survive in the sewers. They made babies. They spread out all over the city. They ate sewer rats. They ate sewer workers. They drank dirty water. They grew to huge sizes. They never saw the sun. They became **albino**. Albino means not having any color. The gators had red eyes. They became blind. They can't survive in the wild. The sun would burn their skin.

Some people believe in **mutant** sewer gators. Mutant means not normal. These gators have been exposed to chemical waste. Companies dump poison into the sewers. This created monsters. An example is a sewer gator with three heads.

People think mutant sewer gators have superpowers.

Chapter Three

MAKING HEADLINES

What is the history of the sewer gators legend? Who is Teddy May? Who is Robert Daley?

The *New York Times* printed stories about alligators. The first story was in 1932. An alligator was found in the Bronx River. The most famous story was printed in 1935. The headline was "Alligator Found in Uptown Sewer." Teenage boys spotted the alligator in the Harlem River. Harlem is in New York City. The alligator was 8 feet (2.4 m) long. The teens pulled it to shore. The alligator snapped. The teens beat it to death with shovels.

City workers said the alligator fell off a boat. People thought there were other alligators. In the 1930s, alligators were seen swimming in the Bronx River. Several dead alligators were found along its banks. Some live ones were caught.

The sewer gators legend started with true stories.

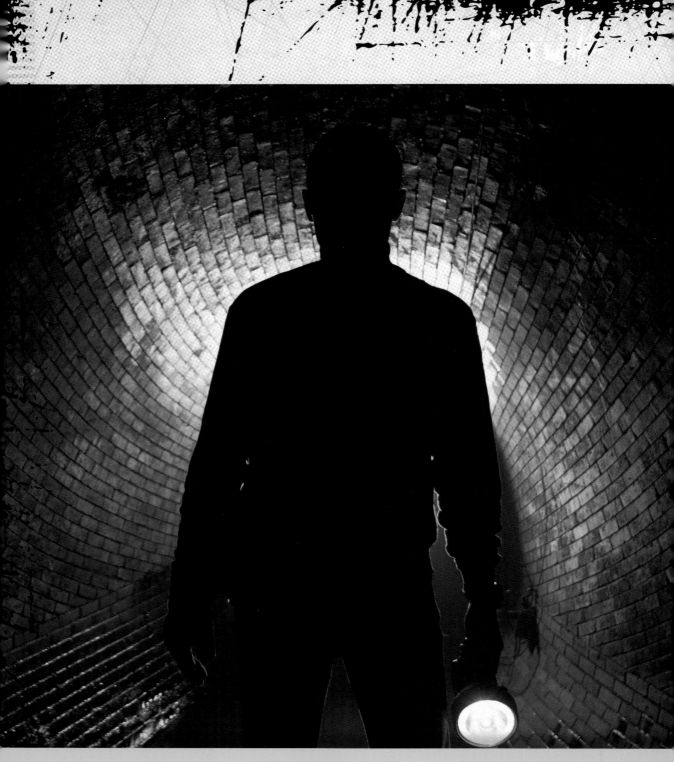

May died in 1960.

Teddy May called himself the "king of the sewers." He didn't believe in sewer gators at first. Then, he investigated. He said he saw them. He saw 2-foot-long (61 cm) gators. The gators lived in small pipes. May said he got rid of them. He poisoned them. He shot at them. He moved them into main lines to be carried out to sea. He did this in the 1930s.

May became part of the sewer gators legend. Some people believed him. Some people didn't. May was known for having an active imagination. He was known to lie.

Daley mentioned how a sewer worker saw a large albino alligator. After that, people hunted for it.

Robert Daley helped the sewer gators story grow. He wrote a book. The book was called *The World Beneath the City*. Daley wrote it in 1959. It was about New York City's sewer system. He wrote about sewer gators. He believed they existed.

He interviewed May. Daley said, "He started telling me about the alligators in the sewer. He wasn't joking. He told me a lot of good stuff. And I accepted it as the truth." May was 84 years old when Daley interviewed him. May's details may have been fuzzy.

REAL-WORLD
CONNECTION

Bucharest is the capital of Romania. Hundreds of people live in the city's sewers. They are called "sewer people." They fled underground in 1989. This is when the Communist government was kicked out. Orphanages were shut down. Orphanages are places where kids without parents live. Many kids were kicked out to the streets. They took shelter in sewer tunnels. The pipes were heated by steam. This kept the area warm. A generation of children grew up in the sewers. The leader said, "Everything we have, we have collected from the garbage. This is how we can live. If not, we would die out on the streets." Sewer people sleep in the sewers at night. They search for food and supplies during the day.

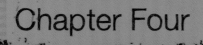

Chapter Four

GATOR FEAR

What is a popular version of the sewer gator story? What do people in London fear?

There are scary stories about sewer gators. This is the basic story: There was a young boy. It was his birthday. He got a special present. He got a baby alligator. He loved it at first. Then, it grew too big. The boy didn't know what to do. He flushed it down the toilet. Years later, he was playing baseball with his friends. He was playing in the street. He lost the baseball. The baseball fell into the sewer. The boy reached his hand into the sewer. He screamed. His arm got ripped off. His alligator ate his arm.

Some think the sewer gators become bloodthirsty.

Sewer gators started in New York City. But the story spread to other cities. London has its own sewer animal stories.

There aren't any sewer gators in London. The English fear giant sewer rats instead. There's a story about rats that are 10 inches (25.4 cm) long. These rats make 200 babies in a year. They're waiting to take over the city.

There's another story about giant sewer pigs. A pregnant pig had an accident. It fell into a sewer. It had babies in the sewer. The pigs ate sewer trash. They became killer sewer pigs.

Sewers are dirty. Visiting sewers can make you sick.

INVESTIGATION TIPS

- Talk to someone who works in sewers. Ask them if they've seen anything in the waters.

- Talk to someone who works with alligators. Ask them where alligators like to live. Ask them how to handle alligators.

- Wash your hands. Do this all the time. Use soap. Scrub under your nails.

- Avoid sewer water. Wear gloves. Wear masks. Wear goggles. Wear bodysuits. Wear rubber boots. Cover any cuts.

- Get a map. Know where the sewer tunnels go. Know how to get out of the sewers. Look for exits.

- Use a gas detection machine. Avoid areas with gas. Avoid explosions.

- Don't eat or drink in the sewers.

Chapter Five

GETTING REAL ABOUT GATORS

What are alligators like? Why can't alligators live in sewers?

Michael Miscione is a historian. He studies New York City. He said, "The concept of alligators in city sewers is a great myth … it has a strong basis in reality."

It makes sense that people are scared of alligators. It also makes sense that alligators are connected with sewers. Alligators are the largest reptiles in North America. They can use tools. They use lures to hunt birds. They balance things on their heads. They have a special blood vessel. This keeps blood away from their lungs. Blood goes to their stomachs. Alligators have strong stomach juices. They can break down meals faster. They can eat a lot.

Alligators have a lot of sharp teeth.

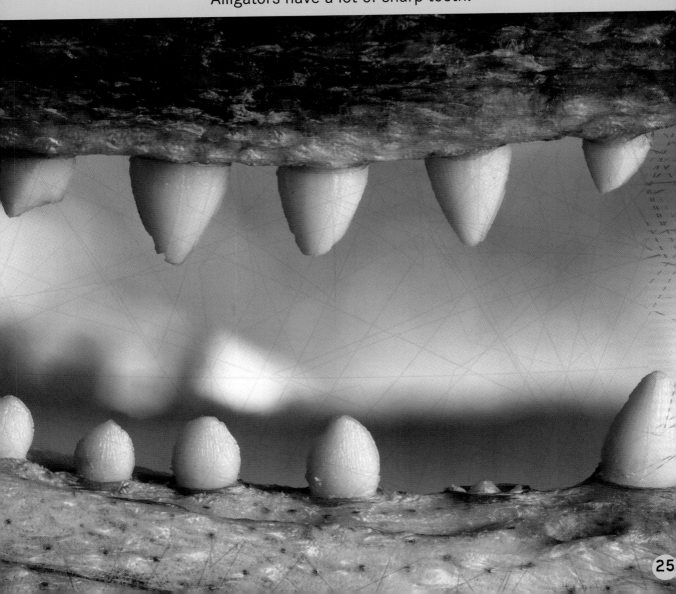

City workers get a lot of calls about sewer gators. They deny they exist.

Their stomachs are like sewers. They eat things whole. Their stomach juices are like lemon juice and vinegar. Meat breaks down in a couple of days. Bones and other hard parts break down in 13 to 100 days. Alligators are tough. They have hard, bony scales. This is like a shield. They have strong blood. Their blood fights against bad germs. They don't get sick easily.

It seems as if alligators could live in sewers. But they can't. People may dump alligators in sewers. But alligators wouldn't live long. First, sewers have a lot of germs. The water is poisonous. Alligators would get sick. They'd die.

Second, sewers don't get enough sunlight. Alligators need sun for their bones. Without sun, their bones would get soft.

EXPLAINED BY SCIENCE

Sewage is wastewater. It's the discarded water from showers, washing machines, sinks, and toilets. A family makes 200 to 300 gallons (757 to 1,135 L) of sewage a day. Sewage can be dangerous. It's dirty. It's smelly. It has bad germs. It can be deadly. It can't get into the drinking water supply. If it does, it would pollute the water. Pollute means to make poisonous. Sewage can cause sickness. It can cause death. Sewage needs to be treated to make it cleaner. It travels through pipes into sewers. Sewers carry sewage to a water treatment building. The sewer system is important to people's lives.

Third, sewers are too cold. Alligators are **cold-blooded**. They take on the temperature of their surroundings. They can take the cold for a while. But they need heat to survive. They can't eat in the cold. They can't break down their food. Their food would rot inside their bodies. This would kill them. Alligators also need heat to lay eggs.

Parents told sewer gator stories. They wanted to scare their children. They didn't want them to play around sewers. Real or not? It doesn't matter. Sewer gators live in people's imaginations.

Sometimes snapping turtles live in sewers.

DID YOU KNOW?

Tom Otterness is an artist. He made a sculpture of a sewer gator. The gator is eating a man. It's in New York City. It's in the subway station. It's part of his "Life Underground" series.

Gray water is sewage from sinks, tubs, showers, dishwashers, and washing machines.

Black water is sewage from toilets.

Ruth Allen works for Animal Care and Control in Brooklyn. She said her center gets about 10 caimans a year.

Sewer gators inspired at least two movies. *Alligator* was made in 1980. It's about a 36-foot-long (11 m) gator. The gator lived in Chicago's sewers. It came out to eat people. *Alligator II: The Mutation* was made in 1991.

Thomas Pynchon wrote a book in 1963. The book is called *V*. It's about an alligator patrol. The patrol's job is to hunt sewer gators.

Baby alligators can be sent through the U.S. mail. They can't be longer than 20 inches (51 cm).

February 9 is Alligators in the Sewers Day. Miscione created the event on the 75th anniversary of the 1935 sighting.

There was an alligator in Paris. In 1984, sewer workers were under a bridge. They found a Nile alligator. The alligator had been eating trash and rats. It was captured. It was named Eleanore. It was put in an aquarium.

CONSIDER THIS!

Take a Position: **Should people have alligators as pets? Argue your point with reasons and evidence.**

Say What? **Sewer gators mix fact and fiction. Explain what is true about sewer gators. Explain what is false about sewer gators.**

Think About It! **Many villains in superhero stories live in sewers. Why do you think that is? What makes sewers such scary places? How do you feel about sewers?**

LEARN MORE

- Fields, Jan. *Hunt for Sewer Gators.* Minneapolis: Calico, 2015.

- Pringle, Laurence, and Meryl Henderson (illus.). *Alligators and Crocodiles! Strange and Wonderful.* Honesdale, PA: Boyds Mill Press, 2009.

- Taylor, Barbara. *Incredible Crocodiles.* Chapel Hill, NC: Armadillo, 2014.

GLOSSARY

albino (al-BYE-noh) not having any color, white

caiman (KAY-men) animal that is in the crocodile family but is related to alligators; often confused for alligators

cold-blooded (kohld-BLUHD-id) animals that take on the temperature of their surroundings, being able to control their body heat by taking in heat from the outside

gators (GAY-turz) short word for "alligators"

mutant (MYOO-tuhnt) not normal, not developing correctly

sewers (SOO-urz) underground pipes or tunnels that carry away wastewater

INDEX

ABOUT THE AUTHOR

Dr. Virginia Loh-Hagan is an author, university professor, former classroom teacher, and curriculum designer. She loves visiting New York City. But she wouldn't want to live there. She lives in San Diego with her very tall husband and very naughty dogs. To learn more about her, visit www.virginialoh.com.